W9-AET-864

I Know Someone with
HIV/AIDS

Elizabeth Raum

Heinemann Library
Chicago, Illinois

www.heinemannraintree.com
Visit our website to find out
more information about
Heinemann-Raintree books.

To order:
☎ Phone 888-454-2279
⌨ Visit www.heinemannraintree.com
to browse our catalog and order online.

Edited by Rebecca Rissman, Dan Nunn,
  and Catherine Veitch
Designed by Steve Mead and Joanna Hinton Malivoire
Picture research by Tracy Cummins
Originated by Capstone Global Library
Printed in the United States of America by
Worzalla Publishing

14 13 12 11 10
10 9 8 7 6 5 4 3 2 1

Library of Congress Cataloging-in-Publication Data
Raum, Elizabeth.
  I know someone with HIV/AIDS / Elizabeth Raum.
    p. cm. — (Understanding health issues)
  Includes bibliographical references and index.
  ISBN 978-1-4329-4554-1 (hc)
  ISBN 978-1-4329-4570-1 (pb)
  1. AIDS (Disease)—Juvenile literature. 2. HIV
infections—Juvenile literature. I. Title.
  RC606.65.R38 2011
  616.97 92—dc22   2010026408

Acknowledgments
Corbis pp. **7** (© David Scharf/Science Faction), **8** (©
Image Source), **10** (© Gareth Brown), **12** (© Edith
Held), **14** (© Jim Craigmyle), **15** (© Simon Jarratt), **29**
(© Tetra Image); Getty Images pp. **16** (Joe Raedle), **21**
(Flynn Larsen), **22** (Stuart O'Sullivan), **24** (Commercial
Eye), **26** (Nathaniel S. Butler/NBAE), **27** (Kevin Winter);
Heinemann Raintree p. **20** (Richard Huchingson);
istockphoto pp **4** (© Chris Schmidt), **6** (© Andrew
Rich), **9** (© Rosemarie Gearhart), **18** (© onebluelight);
Photo Researchers, Inc. p. **11** (Mauro Fermariello);
Shutterstock pp. **5** (© ZouZou), **17** (© Greenland), **25**
(© wow).

Cover photograph of college students on campus
reproduced with permission of Corbis (Corbis Yellow).

We would like to thank Ashley Wolinski and Matthew
Siegel for their invaluable help in the preparation of
this book.

Contents

Some words are printed in bold, **like this**. You can find out what they mean in the glossary.

Do You Know Someone with HIV/AIDS?

Have you heard about HIV/AIDS before? It is a disease that can make people very sick. "HIV" stands for "**Human Immunodeficiency Virus**," and "AIDS" stands for "**Acquired Immune Deficiency Syndrome**."

HIV can affect anyone.

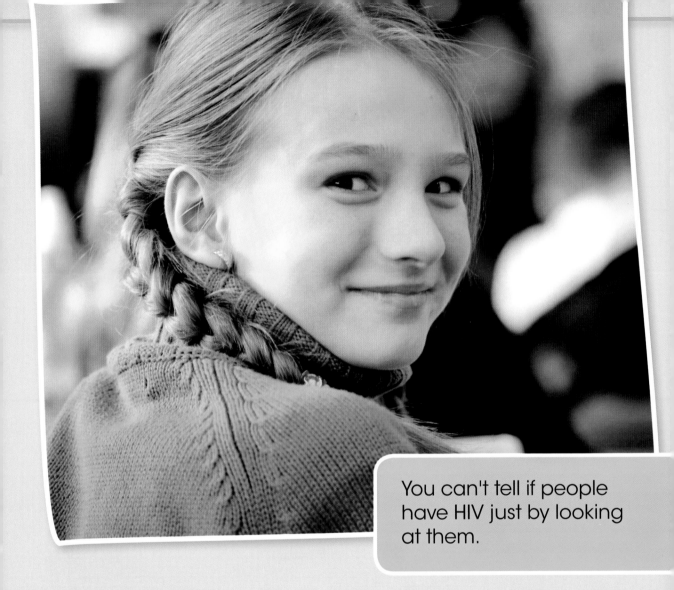

You can't tell if people have HIV just by looking at them.

Many people with HIV are adults or teenagers. Some children have HIV, too. You might know someone with HIV/AIDS.

What Is HIV/AIDS?

The human body is made up of trillions of **cells**. Some cells fight off diseases. Some of these cells are called **T-cells**.

T-cells are like superheroes. They fight disease.

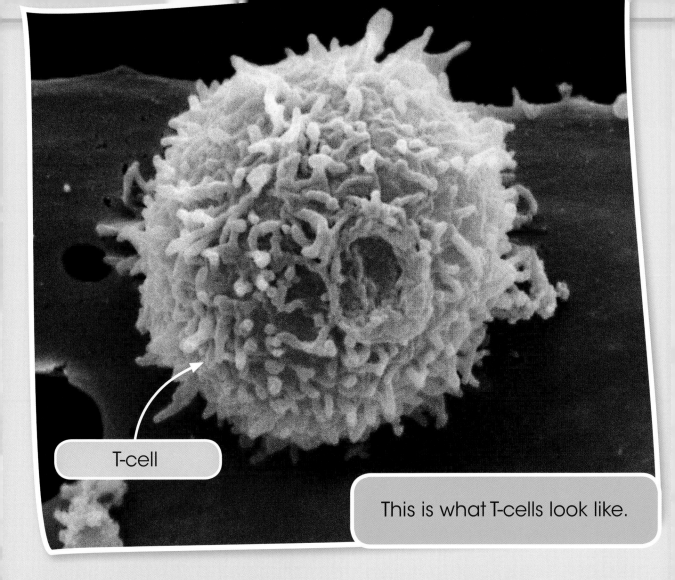

T-cell

This is what T-cells look like.

HIV is an illness that attacks the T-cells that fight disease. When there are not enough cells to fight HIV, doctors say that the person has AIDS.

Mothers and Babies

Most children who have HIV were born with it. Their mothers passed it on when they were **pregnant** or during childbirth.

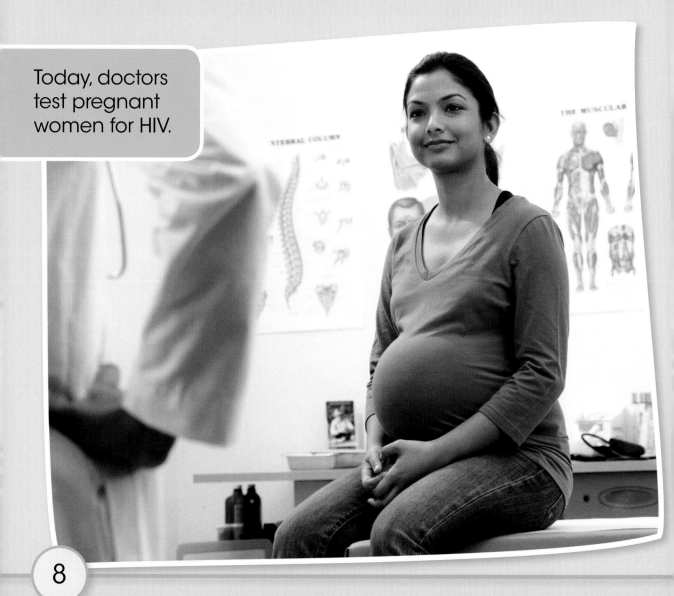

Today, doctors test pregnant women for HIV.

Today, many pregnant women are tested for HIV. If they have it, doctors give them special medicine that protects their babies.

Many babies can be protected from HIV if people get the right help, at the right time.

Blood and HIV

One of the ways people can get HIV is through the blood of someone who has HIV. If someone with a cut on their hand touches the blood of someone with HIV, the virus can spread to them from the other person.

If a friend gets injured and is bleeding, ask an adult to help them.

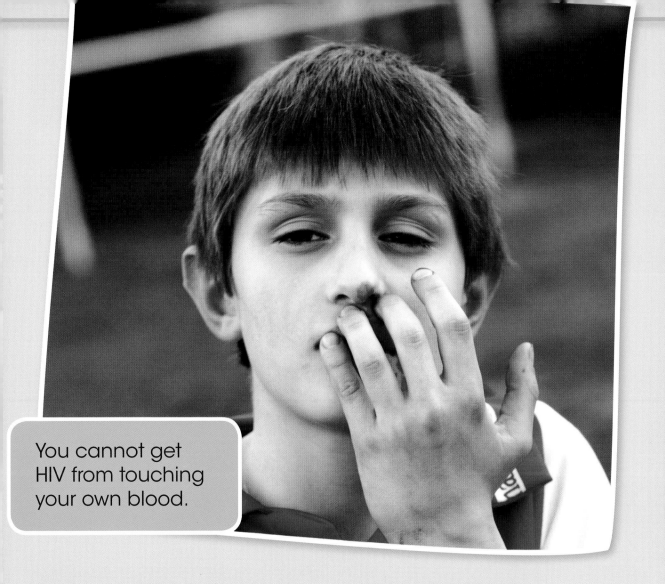

You cannot get HIV from touching your own blood.

Blood may carry other diseases, too. For this reason, you should never touch anyone else's blood. If you see a friend bleeding, it is a good idea to tell an adult.

Will I Get HIV?

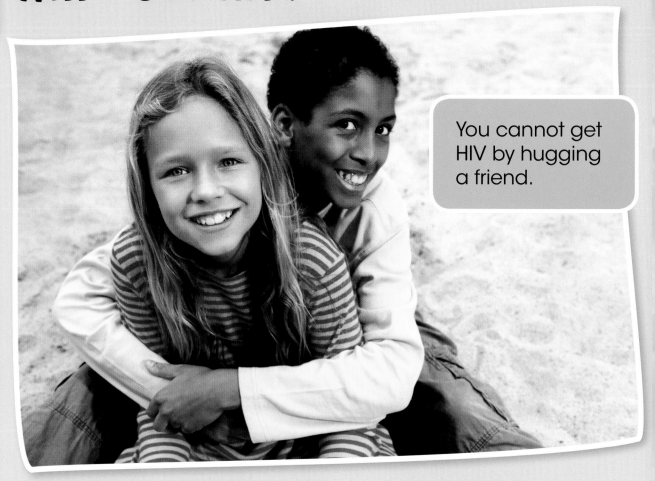

You cannot get HIV by hugging a friend.

You cannot get HIV by playing with your friends at school. You cannot get it by sharing a cookie or by swimming in the same pool.

You cannot get HIV from insect bites or pets. You cannot catch it like a cold. Even if a person with HIV coughs or sneezes near you, you will not catch HIV.

You cannot get HIV from:
- touching someone with HIV
- hugging someone with HIV
- kissing someone with HIV
- sharing food or a drink with someone who has HIV
- shaking hands
- using the same swimming pool
- using the same toilet.

Living with HIV

There is no **cure** for HIV. People who have HIV must take medicine for the rest of their lives.

This scientist is making medicines for people with HIV.

These people are walking to raise money for AIDS **research**.

The medicine helps the **T-cells** in the body keep fighting HIV for longer. Medicines help people with HIV live a longer, healthier life.

Fighting Illness

Adults and children with HIV find it difficult to fight off illnesses. They may become very sick when they have a cold or an ear **infection**. They have to be careful to avoid such illnesses.

Most people with HIV must take medicine every day.

If a friend of yours has HIV, try to stay away from him or her if you are sick.

It can be very easy to spread **germs** from one person to another. If you are sick, try to keep away from your friends until you feel better.

It is important that people with HIV get flu shots and take their medicine to help them keep well. You can help to stop colds and flu from spreading to others by washing your hands often.

Tips for washing your hands:

- Use soap and warm water.
- Scrub for at least 20 seconds (if you do not have a clock, sing the alphabet song).
- Scrub front and back, under your fingernails, and between your fingers.
- Dry with a clean towel or paper towel.

Keeping Healthy

Some children with HIV may have a hard time gaining weight. For others, HIV medicines may make them gain weight. It is important that children with HIV eat a healthy diet.

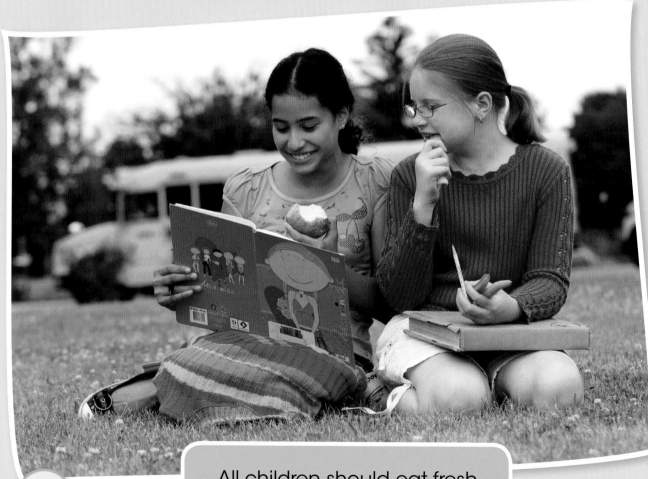

All children should eat fresh fruits and vegetables.

Sleep helps the body fight disease.

Every child should have a healthy diet. Fresh fruits, vegetables, whole grains, and lean meat give us energy and help us stay strong. It is also important for everyone to exercise every day and get enough sleep every night.

Being a Friend

Everyone needs friends. Children with HIV may feel lonely. They may be afraid to tell others that they have HIV. They may worry that other children will stay away from them.

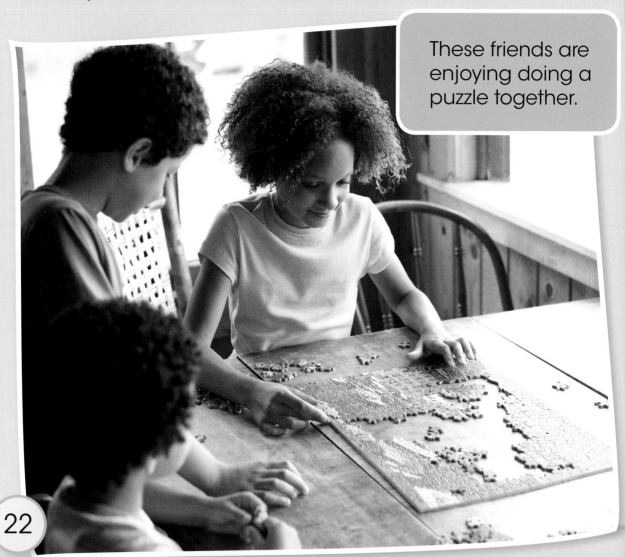

These friends are enjoying doing a puzzle together.

Ways to have fun with your friend:
- put on a play or show
- draw or paint
- do craft projects
- put puzzles together
- play board games
- build with building blocks
- hold doll fashion shows
- race toy cars
- ride bicycles
- read together.

But you know you cannot catch HIV by being near people. You can be with them without worrying about HIV. Listening to music and working on projects together are great ways to show you care.

Helping at Home

Children with HIV often have a parent who has HIV, too. Your friend may have to help care for other members of the family. It is also possible that your friend lives with a grandparent or other relative.

Helping each other with jobs makes life easier.

Friends enjoy time together at school.

Your friend may not want to talk about what is happening at home. Your friend may not be able to invite you over. A good friend understands.

Famous People

Magic Johnson is one of the greatest players in basketball history. In 1991 he learned that he had HIV. Magic Johnson still has HIV, but new medicines have helped him to stay healthy.

Magic Johnson played basketball for the Los Angeles Lakers for many years.

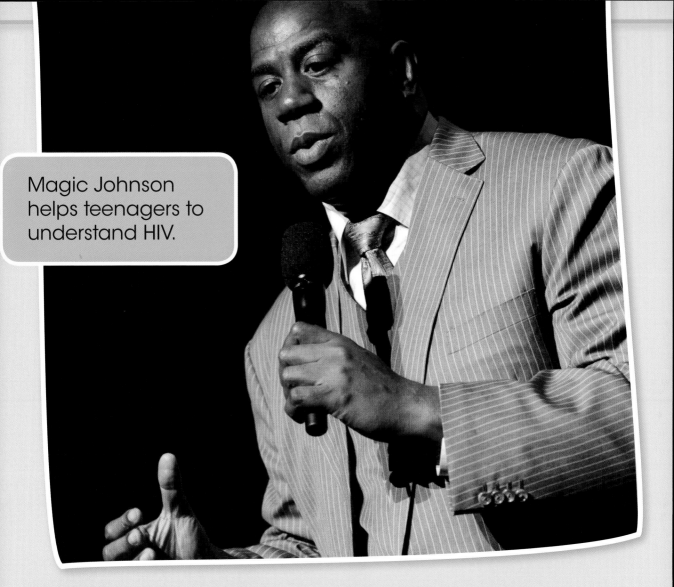

Magic Johnson helps teenagers to understand HIV.

Today, Magic talks to teenagers about how to prevent HIV. He also raises money to help people who have HIV/AIDS and to help doctors find a **cure**.

The Truth About HIV/AIDS

You can catch HIV by hugging and kissing someone who has it.

FALSE! HIV is not like a cold. You cannot catch it by touching someone or breathing the same air.

You can catch HIV by swimming in a public pool or using a public toilet.

FALSE! You cannot even catch HIV by using the same cup or spoon.

Everyone who has HIV will get AIDS.
FALSE! New medicines help to prevent AIDS. People with HIV are living longer and healthier lives.

Glossary

Acquired Immune Deficiency Syndrome disease that makes it hard for the body to fight other illnesses

cell smallest unit that makes up living things

cure medical treatment that makes someone better

germ tiny living thing that can cause disease

Human Immunodeficiency Virus virus that attacks the cells that fight disease and makes people more likely to get sick

infection illness caused by germs

pregnant expecting a baby

research investigate something to find out more information about it

T-cells cells in the body that fight off diseases

Find Out More

Books to Read

Bird, Fiona. *Kids' Kitchen: 40 Fun and Healthy Recipes to Make and Share.* Cambridge, Mass.: Barefoot, 2009.

Claybourne, Anna. *World's Worst Germs (Fusion).* Chicago: Raintree, 2005.

Websites

http://kidshealth.org/kid/stay_healthy/index.html
Visit Kids' Health to learn about health and safety.

http://kidshealth.org/parent/infections/std/hiv.html
Visit Kids' Health to find out about HIV and AIDS.

Index